How to Thrive in South Korea:
97 Tips from Expats

Jackie Bolen

(with advice from 28 expats in Korea)

Jason Ryan (Editor)

Author of: *The Wealthy English Teacher, How to Get a University Job in South Korea* and *39 No-Prep/Low-Prep ESL Speaking Activities*

From: *My Life! Teaching in a Korean University*

Table of Contents

An Introduction to How to Thrive in South Korea

This book is an idea that has been forming in the corners of my mind for years and something that I wish I'd had when I first moved to Korea. I've lived in my adopted home for a decade and during that time, I've met an astounding number of foreigners who were thriving here while I've also met plenty of them who clearly were only surviving, and just barely in some cases. There are even people who've been here a long time still in survival mode, living in tiny apartments, bouncing around from sub-par job to sub-par job and doing nothing to plan for their futures. Conversely, I've met people who, even though they had only been living in Korea for a few months had clearly adapted and were making positive, healthy and sustainable lives for themselves.

This book is a collection of tips from long-term expats who are far beyond surviving and are thriving in Korea. I know most of them personally through work, *KOTESOL* or other networking opportunities while a few of them I've never met in person but we ran across each other in the blog, podcast or websites of the Korean Internet community. They have a lot of wisdom to share with people who are thinking about coming to Korea, have recently just arrived or perhaps even been around for years but want to pick up a few new tips for making their lives better.

I hope you find this book very useful to help you get beyond only surviving South Korea —my goal is that it will be an extremely practical resource that you'll keep going back to for some more inspiration. Make this place your home and thrive. Investing time, money and energy into doing this is something that you'll never regret.

About the Author: Jackie Bolen

I've been living in Korea for the past 10 years and have loved most of my time here. Of course I've had bad days, weeks or even months (mostly involving a terrible hagwon experience that I'd rather forget) but for the most part, Korea is an excellent place to live as an expat if you're able to adapt. This process of adaptation involves figuring out how to make things go smoothly at work, learning how to get along with Koreans, avoiding certain traps that some foreigners fall into, truly making Korea your home, getting out and exploring, and finally making a plan for the future—either in Korea or not.

I'm originally from Canada and came to Korea after college for a bit of adventure and a chance to travel while paying off my students loans. Little did I know that it would become my "real life" and not just a stop along the way but I have no regrets about the way things have turned out. I've been able to work my way up in the job world from a terrible hagwon to a good one, to a decent university job in the countryside, and finally to a great job in Busan.

As far as living in Korea goes, I spend a lot of time cruising around the country on road trips with friends, hanging out in my apartment overlooking the Nakdong River, and going stand-up paddleboarding, biking or hiking whenever I get the chance. During vacations times, I've had some unforgettable adventures around the world that never would have been possible if I had stayed in Canada after university. All that to say—almost anything is possible in Korea and your life can be whatever you want it to be.

If you like this book, please leave a review on *Amazon* and don't forget to check out my other books at the same time:

The Wealthy English Teacher is a book in which you can learn all about finances for English teachers. If you are interested in getting the most awesome job in South Korea which is working at a university—please check out *How to Get a University Job in South Korea.*

Jackie Bolen around the Internet

ESL Speaking (www.eslspeaking.org)

My Life! Teaching in a Korean University (www.teachinginkoreanuniversity.com)

Twitter: @bolen_jackie

Website: www.jackiebolen.com

How to Thrive: Work

Like anywhere, a good job can go a long way towards ensuring that you have a happy life in South Korea. Conversely, a terrible job will be hard to overcome and you will likely feel pretty miserable in the rest of your life away from work as well. Before you even come to Korea, you need to make sure that the job you take is a decent one and then once you start working, you'll want to make sure things go smoothly. Here are some tips to help make your work life—and by extension, the rest of your life—as awesome as it can be.

Be Flexible

In Korea everything happens last minute—I call this the "bbali-bbali" syndrome (bbali = "fast" in Korean) and what it means is that at work you need to be flexible and roll with the punches. Here are some examples of things that have happened to me:
- getting a new class to teach less than five minutes before it was set to start
- being told about a school dinner as people were walking out the door
- finding out about some urgent paperwork that needed to be submitted less than 24 hours before the deadline

These are only three examples that I thought of off the top of my head but I could come up with countless more things. If you're the type of person who needs to plan everything far in advance and can't handle last minute changes, then you'll have a really tough time in Korea. What I find really helpful is to repeat this mantra in my head when the bbali-bbali things happen, "Serenity now!" Then I laugh to myself and go about my normal chilled-out mode of operation. In the end, the Koreans around you will always pull through with what needs to get done, even if they go about it in a different manner than you would.

Be Reliable

Teaching in Korea is a real job—it's not a vacation. If you're working at a hagwon, your boss is trying to make money and run a business so they need you to show up each and every single day. If you work at a public school or university, the profit motive may not be there, but you'll severely inconvenience your co-workers and administrators if you aren't ready for all your classes. By showing up, I mean ready to teach with a lesson plan of sorts and a smile on your face. Even if you aren't the best teacher (and who is in their first year?), as long as you're reliable and try your best to help the students, you'll make it.

Work Hard

Koreans put in some of the longest hours of anyone in the world and it's really normal for employees in the big companies like *Samsung* to go into work at 9am and then finish the day at 7pm. After that, there are often mandatory work dinners or meetings with clients. While you won't experience this extreme, you will be expected to work hard for your money. This can include things like proofreading for brochures or tests, planning lessons, phoning students, doing report cards or going to opening and closing ceremonies. This is a normal part of life in Korea and unless they are really unreasonable requests, you should just do them without complaint.

Let me tell you a story from when I was working at a sketchy hagwon (private language institute) for my first job in Korea. Due to the sketchiness of it, I didn't have the best attitude towards working there and whenever they asked me to do some extra little thing, I'd usually say no. The relationship continued to deteriorate and the whole regretful year ended badly with trips to the labor board, an apartment eviction and other such terrible things. In retrospect, I should have said yes to all those things that would have cost me little in terms of energy and time in order to maintain a positive relationship and I'm sure things would have ended much more amicably. In Korea, relationships are everything and whatever you can do to maintain smooth ones can go a long way to helping you thrive instead of just survive in Korea.

Another area that you should work hard at is preparing your lessons. I've heard plenty of teachers brag over the years about how they just walk into class, ask the students what page they're on, and then "teach." Except that it's really, really hard to have consistently great classes if you do this and your students will be served far better if you plan ahead. At the very least, you could consider these questions which will take you less than five minutes per class:

1. How will you introduce the target language? A reading? A listening exercise? A story? A worksheet?

2. What will you write on the board?

3. What controlled practice activity will you do? What page in your book? Another resource? Is it student-centered? How will you provide feedback?

4. What freer practice activity will you do? Is it student-centered? Are students active and engaged? How will you provide feedback?

5. What will you do if you have some extra time left at the end of class?

6. Do you need any supplementary materials?

7. Follow-up or review in the next class?

Relationships are More Important than Contracts

Relationships are the most important thing in Korea and you should do everything you can to maintain positive ones. In contrast, contracts generally aren't worth the paper they're written on, especially if you're working at a hagwon where there might be discrepancies related to working hours, overtime pay, vacation time, pension and health care. Public schools and universities are often better at following contracts, but there is vague language that can be understood in a variety of ways. For example, things related to apartment maintenance, vacation days and sick days are often wide open to interpretation.

Where does that leave you? Basically, you're stuck working at a place that might not necessarily honor the contract that you've signed. It should lead you to focus a lot of your energy on maintaining a positive relationship with your hagwon boss, university administrators or your public school co-teachers.

I'll tell you about a mistake that foreign teachers in Korea often make. There's usually a clause in contracts about how the school is responsible to provide housing for the teacher. Except that there sometimes isn't a desk, rice cooker or shower curtain provided because the school doesn't think they're vital, while the foreign teacher does. Instead of just going out and buying any of these cheap things which can be easily picked up second-hand, the foreign teacher complains to anyone who will listen. Their Korean co-workers and bosses get sick of them complaining and buy the thing for them but that relationship is burned and will be really difficult to repair. Was it worth the 20,000 Won?

Another example is about what happens when something in the apartment breaks. Maybe it's the microwave or the washing machine that needs a small repair of 50,000 Won or less. The foreign teacher tells their boss or co-worker who sends someone over to fix it and then the teacher has to pay the repairman. The teacher brings the receipt to school and insists that they pay it. The school says no and that the teacher should pay because they're the one that broke it. It blows up into a big issue and while the teacher may get the money, that relationship is damaged beyond repair—the teacher should really not be surprised when they don't get their contract renewed or their hagwon tries to rip them off. Always think carefully about complaining to your school, especially about housing stuff and if it's just a small amount of money, pay it yourself.

Appearance

If you want to teach in Korea, you need to think carefully about your appearance. Do your best to look like a teacher which means wearing appropriate attire, ditching the backpack, getting a messenger bag or briefcase and grooming yourself like any teacher would in your home country. Also think carefully about your picture in the application package —you should get it professionally done, and wear a business suit (men and women). Men should be clean shaven and if you have facial hair make sure it's trimmed neatly. Women should wear make-up and if you get professional shots done consider going to have your hair and make-up done professionally at a salon before your photo session. Your portrait, can, and often will be, the deciding factor on whether you get an interview, and in particular the job.

Don't just Fill the Time

We've all been there when we're new to teaching—a one hour class with no book or only one page that we've been assigned to teach. There's that moment of panic when we wonder how we could possibly fill that hour with, well, nothing. So we play Hangman and perhaps a round of Bingo. Teaching is not *just* talking to your students or playing Bingo and Hangman—there's plenty more to it if you want your students to actually improve their skills. Check out the Teaching Resources section at the back of this book to help you get started.

Get Qualified

If you want to stick with the English teaching gig for at least a few years, it can certainly help open some doors if you get more formally qualified. Here are some ways that you can do this:

-complete a master's degree in education, TESOL, or English

-get a CELTA or DELTA certificate

-get certified to administer and grade popular exams such as TOIEC speaking or IELTs

-get a teaching certification and license from your home country, which opens up the option of teaching at international schools

-get published, formally or informally

-make a name for yourself through blogging, social media or other online ventures

-present at conferences and make sure you get certificates proving that you did so

-volunteer with an English teaching organization (for example, *KOTESOL*) and accept positions with increasing responsibility

Get Better Jobs

Let's face it—hagwon jobs are often terrible. They involve long hours (30 classroom hours per week, low vacation time (2 weeks) and the worst part is that your boss is often trying to rip you off on things like pay, taxes, pension, healthcare and housing. Public schools are better in that you have fewer teaching hours, more vacation and you usually won't get ripped off but you can often have substandard housing and low pay. The best jobs by far are the corporate and university ones, but these require some serious qualifications such as a master's degree, years of experience and of course the right connections to get you an introduction. For some solid advice on how to get a university job in South Korea, check out this book: *How to Get a University Job in South Korea.* Above all, remember that the best jobs are never advertised so make networking a serious priority in your life.

Think beyond your first year in Korea and make a plan to move up in the world. Maybe you work at a terrible hagwon—make a plan for how to get a public school job or better hagwon job. Perhaps you work at a public school in the lowest salary tier—make a plan to move up into a higher one or get a university job. There is always a better job to get in the teaching English world in Korea and if you can get a prime one, it will make your life far better. More pay, less work, less stress, better students—who doesn't want that?

Networking is Huge

I once asked teachers in a *Facebook* group that I'm a part of how they got their university jobs in Korea and 50% of them said through friends or networking. Most hagwons (the good ones you want to work at) and universities prefer to hire someone already vetted by a current employee. Here are some networking tips.

My Four Rules of Networking

My first rule of networking is don't be creepy, obnoxious, immature, lazy, unethical or unprofessional because nobody will want to be your co-worker. I guarantee that people will not recommend you to work at their university or good hagwon because you will be like a black mark against them if your behavior offends people.

The second rule of networking is to go where the university teachers can be found. You will find very few university teachers at events like bus tours for newbies (for example, *Adventure Korea*), the Mud Festival, *Thursday Party*, scavenger hunts, or the local dance club. University teachers tend to be a bit of an older crowd and so you are more likely to run into them in these kinds of places: an English Church, language exchange group, book club, board game club or expat pubs that attract an older crowd. When you meet a university teacher, just be normal. Do not get all excited and try to go in too early for the kill. I recommend actually talking to that person like they're a human being and not just a university job vending machine.

Next, get involved with *KOTESOL*. By involved, I mean actively because this is how you form friendships and garner a good reputation. A good way to do this is to attend local chapter meetings, which happen once a month or join a Special Interest Group (SIG). At my local *KOTESOL* chapter meeting in Busan, about 50% of the people who regularly attend work at a university. Attend the annual international and national conferences and use your time wisely. Introduce yourself to presenters and be approachable and friendly. Make an effort to network and meet some new people. Also consider volunteering your time and talents; *KOTESOL* is entirely run by volunteers and it is an excellent way to meet lots of people that work in a variety of places. Of course, you should try to get business cards from people that you meet and follow-up with a short email saying that you appreciated talking to them, etc.

Finally, *Facebook* is an excellent place to network. Consider joining the general

KOTESOL group, as well as your local *KOTESOL* chapter group. Also join the Foreign Teachers in Korean Universities group on *Facebook*. Be active in these groups and carefully develop your personal and professional image as a respectful, intelligent person who contributes helpful ideas to discussions. When you have an interesting discussion with someone, perhaps send them a private message and a friend request, but do not be overly eager and forget to use good social etiquette.

Become a Professional - Rob Dickey

Whether you are 22 or 62, no one can afford an empty year on their resume because the world is just too competitive. Koreans perceive this differently, and new university graduates would rather appear to be unemployed ("white hands") than to take a job beneath their dignity—at least for their paperwork! They can always claim to have been studying independently!

There are two aspects to professionalism: the first one if you want to make teaching a career and the other one if you don't. First: start your teaching career right. Whichever teaching job you are in, however they treat you, take class preparation and classroom performance seriously. Your next job may come from those who see you in your current job and your students deserve your best. Recognize that in Korea, you are a teacher 24/7, so your dress and behavior off-campus can impact perceptions of your professionalism. Participating in professional/academic societies is an excellent way to demonstrate to others that you consider yourself a professional.

If English teaching isn't your long-term future, OK. But be a teacher, not a vacationer who teaches to pay the bills. Start working towards whatever that non-teaching future may be. Read books. Practice your skills. Maintain contacts in the professional community (discussion lists, Facebook groups, alumni associations). Be ready to hit the ground running when your teaching term ends. Don't make this a blank year on your resume that sets you back when you return home. You will just be a year older, and further from the most current education versus those you will be competing against for your next job.

About Rob Dickey:

Rob is a past president of Korea TESOL (*KOTESOL*), a 20+ year resident of Korea who teaches various "content" courses along with "pure" English courses. See more about content teaching at *Content English (www.content-english.org)*.

Get Involved with *KOTESOL* - Robert M. Kim

After being laid off at two ESL teaching jobs in community colleges back home in America, I applied to teach in Korea and was offered my first job in Korea at Duksung Women's University. I did a Google search to see if there were any English teacher organizations, discovered KOTESOL, and as soon as I started teaching at Duksung, I began to get involved by attending Seoul chapter workshops.

At first, I struggled with teaching in Korea because I thought that since the students had been learning English since elementary school, they would have a high beginning to low intermediate level of English. To my surprise, they did not. Also, they were not used to any communicative or student-centered learning activities and the majority of the pupils had no background in learning how to write essays or paragraphs in English.

Due to this experience, I used KOTESOL as a means for my growth. I learned about various aspects of the Korean education system such as how it is form-focused, accuracy driven teacher-centered learning rather than fluency driven student-centered learning. Over the years, I've hosted workshops in various KOTESOL conferences and chapter workshops and have even had articles published in The English Connection on topics such as teaching reading, dealing with Korean culture in the classroom, and teaching writing.

Over time, I've experienced professional prosperity teaching EFL in Korea. After switching from Duksung Womens University to Kyonggi University (Suwon Campus) in 2008, I've widened my professional network with like-minded professionals who are devoted to continual professional and personal growth in the ELT field. Likewise, I have helped get a small KOTESOL chapter in Gyeonggi-Yongin up and running.

Overall, I have experienced things that I never thought would happen. I am very active with a vibrant network of English teachers around me. Likewise, I have learned new things to help me advance my career, such as web editing skills and new ways to hone my pedagogical craft. Not bad for someone who experienced a tough layoff back in 2006!

About Robert M. Kim:

Robert is a second generation Korean-American who currently teaches at Kyonggi University. He is a proud member of *KOTESOL* and has served the following roles in the Gyeonggi-Yongin *KOTESOL* Chapter: president, vice-president, webmaster, and immediate past president.

It's All About Saving Face

Korea is a shame-based culture which means that it's extremely important to save face and not make someone appear badly in front of others. This means that things like public arguments, shaming a student for bad behaviour or pointing out someone's error in public is a big no-no. Just think about whether or not any action you do will embarrass someone around you. If the answer is yes, then consider your actions carefully. It's easiest just to smile, go with the flow and think about how everyone can look like a star.

However, in the classroom this shame based culture can make language learning quite difficult because it's hard to master a language without making mistakes. I try to remind my students of this almost every class and tell them that the more mistakes they're making, the more they're going to improve. As a teacher, you'll need to tread carefully with how you do error correction and as a general rule, it's fine to point at an error to a student privately, but if you're going to do it publicly, say something like, "Someone said XYZ, but the correct way is ABC."

Sick Days

Korea is a little bit ridiculous with sick days; there's no such thing as staying at home with a cold or flu and the only time you should miss a day of work is if you're actually sleeping overnight in the hospital. This is why you'll see plenty of people hanging around outside hospitals dressed in hospital garb with something like a broken arm or leg, which in our home countries would get taken care of in a matter of hours.

Even though there are sick days in your contract, you aren't expected to actually use them. None of your Korean co-workers will and they'll never miss a day of work unless they're on their deathbeds. If you call in sick, it's these Korean co-workers who have to pick up the slack and they'll likely end up resenting you. Come contract renewal or reference letter time, you probably won't like the result if you use more than one or two days a year.

Be Intentional about Getting to Know People at Work

I asked some of my friends what their top tip for thriving instead of surviving in South Korea is and one of them mentioned that he's intentional about getting to know people at work—co-workers, students (he's a university teacher), the administrators, and professors in other departments. I definitely agree with him on this one because it makes work life much more pleasant if you see at least a few friendly faces every day. The people that we work with often make less than stellar jobs tolerable and we should do our best to cultivate relationships with our co-workers, both foreign and Korean.

Collaborate with Co-Workers

Teaching can be a pretty lonely thing sometimes—it's just us and the students, especially if you work at a university and don't have something like a shared staff room. Your daily life as a teacher, however, doesn't have to be isolated and it can be encouraging to collaborate with the people you work with. Things like a shared *Dropbox* or *Google Drive* can go a long way towards facilitating this. Even if your school doesn't have this set up already, take some initiative and make it happen. Hopefully people will use and appreciate it and you'll get some encouragement in the process.

Respect your Bosses

Korean society is a hierarchical one and whole books have been written on this topic but I'll give you the most basic of overviews. When a Korean meets someone for the first time, it's really important that they're able to place that person as senior, junior or equal to them (in terms of social rank and authority) because how they address them in Korean (more or less politely) depends on it. This is why things like age, job titles, hometowns and educational backgrounds matter far more in Korea than they do in our home countries.

What this means for you is that you need to respect your boss and strive to maintain friendly relations at all times. These tips will go a long way to assist you in this:

1. Always let your boss pay for anything if you go out together. It's ridiculous and insulting to even try to pay.

2. Greet your boss warmly the first time you see him or her that day with a smile, bow of the head and "Annyeong hasaeyo (Hello/good morning/afternoon/evening, etc.).

3. Always be professional at work. NEVER talk badly about your boss to your co-workers, Korean or foreign, but especially Korean. They are likely far more loyal to your boss than to you and word *will* get back to your boss.

4. Strive for only positive interactions. I call this my, "Fly under the radar policy," where I try to never interact with my bosses for anything that could be thought of as negative. This is sometimes impossible but it's a good goal to strive for during your time in Korea.

Research Jobs Thoroughly

Having a good job is the number one thing that can make your life in Korea enjoyable; conversely, a bad job will likely make you pretty miserable. Taking this into account, it's worth every second of time invested to vet a job offer before deciding to take it. This advice mostly applies to hagwon jobs since public school and universities are generally above board and you don't have to worry too much about getting ripped off by them.

Ten years ago, there were a few sites like *The Hagwon Blacklist* but these days, most teachers find the expat *Facebook* group for the city they're considering teaching in and ask about a hagwon's reputation on there. You'll usually get a response from someone who works there, has worked there, or who knows someone that works or worked there. Another place to ask around is on the *ESL Cafe* Korea forums but be wary because much of the information you get there tends to be quite negative towards things.

Another good way to vet a place is to talk to the foreign teacher that works there. But be careful because this can be somewhat unreliable because that teacher wants their airfare and bonus money so they might be reluctant to tell you the truth about their place and anger their boss. A safer bet is to try to get the contact information for a former teacher (or two or three) who has finished a contract within the past couple years. They have far less to lose than the current teachers. If nobody has finished contracts or the school is reluctant to give out any contact information—that's quite a bad sign and it's likely a place that should be avoided.

Hagwons are Businesses First, Places of Education Second

Many foreigners come to Korea to work at a hagwon with the idea that they're going to be working at a "school." While this is partly true, you need to remember that it's a business first and that all decisions will be made from this perspective. Keeping the moms happy is the hagwon owner's highest calling, not ensuring that the kids learn English—or that you are happy with your job conditions. Keep this in the back of your mind and understand that many decisions get made from a business perspective, not an educational one.

Co-Teachers and Department Secretaries are not Concierges

During my time in Korea, I've heard people talk about things they had their co-teachers (public schools), co-workers (hagwons) or department secretaries (universities) do for them. These things were way beyond the normal kind of stuff that would even very loosely fit into their job description and included things like dealing with mislabelled packages at customs, buying plane tickets, organizing a truck to move a couch, talking to landlords, signing for cell-phones, and the list goes on.

In my experience, it's far better to deal with personal stuff yourself and only ask work colleagues for help with work tasks or issues. If you keep asking the Koreans around you to do something that isn't really their job, they will soon feel used and that relationship will not be as awesome as it could be. Instead, you could learn Korean and deal with stuff yourself, find English speaking services, or hire someone (a university student) to help you with life stuff or ask a Korean friend or long-term expat. If you ask a friend to help you, be sure to reward them with things like dinner or small gifts so they'll feel appreciated. You could also try spreading around the requests to a few different friends so that no single person shoulders the whole burden of your life! They're busy with their own lives already.

Three Keys to Success at Work - Aaron Shayne

In my experience, there are three key ways to thrive in Korea. First, it's important to create positive relationships with your co-workers. Bring in some food or small presents to work every few weeks and if your co-workers are interested, take them out for dinner or drinks. These relationships are instrumental to your happiness and your professional progress while you are in the EFL field.

Second, make sure to stay organized. You should have a folder with all your important information (updated resume, university transcripts, reference letters, etc.) ready to present to a potential employer at a moment's notice. This will save you a lot of time and misery the next time you are looking for a job or have to make a trip to the immigration office.

Finally, be prepared and professional. Take time to carefully plan your lessons and dress to impress. Appearance matters but it matters even more in Korea. Wearing a suit and tie or at least a collared shirt and slacks to work every day will make you stand out among your co-workers. There is a lot more to thriving in Korea but building positive relationships, staying organized and being professional are a good start.

About Aaron Shayne:

Aaron is a professor at Silla University in Busan. He holds a Master's in Education with a focus on ESOL. He has been teaching a variety of English courses in Korea for five years.

How to Thrive: Things to Avoid

When you go to live and work in a new place, it's pretty easy to get stuck in the cycle of doing the same things all the time. If they're healthy things like cultivating friendships, learning Korean, exercising, or planning for your future, it can be a good cycle to get into. It's pretty easy however to get stuck in a cycle filled with bad stuff that is best avoided. Here are some things that will not get you far if your goal is to thrive and not just survive in South Korea.

Avoid the Vacation Haze - Sara Peterson

The key to thriving in your new country is making it your home. Some expats live like they're in a post-college, permanent vacation haze. They may end up finding themselves stranded in a foreign country, out of a job with no money and no future plans if they aren't careful. Sure, it's fun drinking and going out every night but you'll never truly feel settled. You have to commit to your new country, even if it's just for a year. Be the best teacher you can be. Make your apartment a place you like to come home to. Build relationships with your colleagues. Make an effort to understand the culture. Study the language. Save money. Set long-term goals and work to improve yourself personally and professionally. At the end of your contract you'll find that you have grown, are in good financial shape, and ready for whatever step you choose next.

About Sara Peterson:

Sara is an assistant professor at Silla University in Busan, South Korea. She has a Master's in Education and has been teaching and researching EFL in Korea for 5 years. She can be found at *Teach in Korea (www.teachinkoreablog.wordpress.com).*

Avoid the Expat Bars

I love a good expat bar. There's all the greasy food, imported beer and English speaking staff that I could possibly want. Except that there's a whole lot more to Korea than what you'll find there and your experience will be much better if you spend it out in the real world, doing things and enjoying activities rather than drowning your culture shock or loneliness in another beer. Plus, expat bars are the most expensive places to drink in Korea—it's way cheaper and just as fun to go to some of the local Korean pubs, especially the ones around universities. If you really want to hang out at the expat bars, be sure to set a limit for how many times a week you want to do this. Moderation and balance make for a healthy and happy life.

Avoid Drinking Too Much

Koreans love drinking and you'll often see news articles mentioning Korea as in the top five or ten nations in the world in terms of alcohol consumption. Koreans really do like to get their drink on, as do most of the foreigners and it can be really, really easy to end up drinking four or five nights a week before you even quite realize what is happening.

The best way to avoid this is to get involved with activities that do not involve alcohol such as a book club that meets at a coffee shop, board game clubs, hiking or biking groups, English speaking churches, etc. In addition, it's helpful to cultivate friendships with people who for whatever reason don't drink as much as many of the Koreans and expats do.

Avoid *ESL Cafe*

If you hang around the Korea forums on *ESL Cafe* too much, it's possible to end up bitter, angry, depressed and hating your life in Korea because it seems to be filled mostly with unhappy people. There are plenty of other places to get information these days—blogs and many of the *Facebook* groups are much more positive and productive. Or, build a network with other teachers in Korea and post on your *Facebook* wall if you have a question and you'll likely get some helpful responses.

Avoid the Korea Haters

Korea is not an easy place to live so it's really useful to surround yourself with helpful, supportive and positive people. These people are indeed around and many of the ones that I know have contributed to this book but you won't find them by looking in the usual places. They're often out enjoying all that Korea has to offer and won't be found in the bars or the online forums.

The people that you should stay away from are the haters. These are the people that hate anything and everything Korea. They don't like the food. They hate the people. They can't read Korean. Their job sucks. They think it's dirty and smelly. If you're not careful, this negativity will start to seep into your mind.

Avoid the Overpriced Western Restaurants

I know one guy who came to Korea for the first time and ate at Outback Steakhouse *5-6* times a week for the first couple months he was here. Not only was it extremely unhealthy, but it was very expensive too and he ended up burning through his reserve pool of money in no time and was scrimping and saving until his first paycheck. The Western chains like TGIFridays and Outback are rip-offs and should be avoided, especially considering that the food is kind of sub-par. I'd way rather go out for some Korean BBQ (or a number of other Korean meals) which is far cheaper, healthier and just as delicious. Cooking at home is also an excellent option!

Avoid the "This is How We Do It at Home" Mentality

I have seen all kinds of ridiculous things that expats try to do when they first come to Korea including insisting on giving children failing marks on their tests at hagwons (remember —it's a business), putting up shower curtains in their wet bathrooms, insisting that their school buy them a clothes dryer, using sick days and/or expecting to be paid for unused ones (remember—they should never be taken). Just because that's what would happen in your home country doesn't mean that's how it happens in Korea. You need to get over this and just accept it for what it is—different, but not necessarily better or worse; it is what it is. Don't complain and don't be angry—get used to it as fast as possible and you will be well on your way to thriving instead of just surviving.

How to Thrive: Living in Korea

Know What Resources are Out There - Sharon Couzens

I'm a planner. The best tip I could give someone coming to Korea is to know where to get what you need. There are a number of good websites out there, such as Waygook and Korea4Expats where you can find information about everything from how to sort your trash to hospitals. Facebook has tons of groups for teachers in Korea—if you find one, you can find all.

If you're looking to buy things for your apartment, try Craigslist or the Yongsan Flea Market on Facebook. Buying and selling items in Korea might be different than what you're used to back home but I've done it hundreds of times and never had a problem. In Korea, if you're buying something you transfer the money and the seller will mail it to you.

Knowing a few key phone numbers will help. If you call 120, someone can translate for you. 1330 is the 24-hour tourist hotline. They'll tell you where things are but will not translate for you. In case of an emergency call 1339 and they'll connect you to an English speaking operator. If you have legal issues, the Labor Board at 1350 can give you advice. You can also get help on the Facebook groups: LOFT: Legal Office for Foreign Teachers and PALS: Practice Advice for Legal Situations.

Learning to be independent in a foreign country where you might not speak the language is a lot easier nowadays. You can find so much information online and there are people you can call if you need help so it's easier than ever to thrive in Korea.

About Sharon Couzens:

Sharon has lived abroad since January 2002 and has been teaching in Korea for over five years. You can find her online at *TEFL Tips (www.tefl-tips.com)* and *The Ultimate Peru List (www.theultimateperulist.blogspot.com).*

Build a Large Network ASAP - Val Hamer

Having a range of people to spend time with makes such a difference, and the best bit is you get to meet so many folk you'd never come across at home. Rather than looking for a soul mate focus on meeting loads of folk. Eventually you'll find people you become closer to, but a variety of contacts makes life interesting. Some ways to do this are:

Say yes to pretty much every (non-sketchy) invitation you get in the first few weeks/months in South Korea. Even if it means working out how to use public transport to attend, or you're tired, or you won't know many of the people who will be there. Facebook makes it easy to connect so don't be shy about getting usernames or emails.

Look for local foreigner information groups on Facebook. Most areas have at least one, and these often have details on events in your area. Google around for details of interesting 'MeetUp' groups within travelling distance, or if you like group trips look for Adventure Korea.

About Val Hamer:

Val has been successfully making friends in South Korea since 2007. Writer, coffee-addict and lover of puzzles—she tweets @farawayhammer.

Find the Group for You - Jennifer Booker Smith

For me, the key to a happy and successful life in Korea was getting involved with a group of like-minded people. There are dozens of expat groups for every interest, but if you can't find a group that suits, create one! For me, joining KOTESOL, and getting involved not only kept me motivated to improve as an educator, but also introduced me to some great friends and provided an excellent network for unadvertised jobs. I was also an irregular participant at Stitch n Bitch and a hiking group. I'm much more a recluse than a social butterfly, but spending time with other native speakers was an important way for me to recharge each weekend. I also had a sounding board when I needed to vent about work, and listening to others vent reminded me that my problems weren't unique or particularly bad.

Obviously, you can sit at any bar in Itaewon and complain about your job, but doing something constructive at the same time was the key for me. Your time in Korea is what you make it. Do you really want to spend 52 consecutive weekends getting drunk and complaining about your boss?

About Jennifer Booker Smith:

Jennifer holds a Master's of Education in TESOL. She taught in South Korea from 1998-2013, during which time she held a variety of positions on the *KOTESOL* Seoul Chapter executive in addition to serving as secretary of the national council for two years. In her free time, she hikes, runs, and knits.

Be Open - Ben Weller

For me, thriving in Korea or anywhere else is all about openness. I try to keep my eyes, ears, heart and mind open to everything around me. I watch what people do, how they do it, and I keep myself open to trying new things and new ways of living. Being open, even just a little bit, goes a long way. Korean people, and most people I think, are impressed when foreigners in their midst make even the tiniest effort to learn, understand, and adapt. This garners respect, and being respected will make you happier and better able to navigate the intricacies and obstacles of life in Korea.

About Ben Weller:

Ben has taught at Silla University in Busan for five years, while also building a successful freelance photography career, working for major news and commercial clients. His next move is to Nagoya, Japan. Visit his website at *Ben Weller Photography (www.benweller.photoshelter.com).*

Get Married - Anonymous

Whatever degree of success I have had in Korea is really tied up with my marriage.

When I came to Korea I knew I wanted to teach (though at that time, not necessarily English). Additionally, having lived in Europe as a Peace Corps volunteer for two years, I was confident I could gain conversational level competence in Korean. Thus, I figured I could use Korean as a way to build a social network. That certainly worked.

After getting married I decided that since I wanted to teach, why not English? Why not stay in Korea as long as possible? That meant doing an online MSEd. I felt a little guilty about doing an online master's as if I were cheating by doing it online. Thus, that motivated me to supplement my online program with KOTESOL workshops/meetings. After missing some excellent opportunities to serve as a workshop facilitator during my time in the Peace Corps, I learned one key lesson: if you want a leadership spot in an institution you need to strive for it early. Long story short, that attitude got me appointed as secretary for Busan-Gyeongnam KOTESOL. Since that time I have held at least a half dozen roles in KOTESOL and I went through a similar process with Toastmasters.

On the language front, while my speaking surely has limitations, I have read substantially in the Korean language and have made many friends which will supply me with a lifetime of incredible memories. It has also helped in my job, as I can better understand the source of students' errors, have a somewhat better grasp of Korean culture, as well as increased empathy with foreign language learners. The above activities have assisted greatly in helping me land a job, and eventually getting promoted to NET head teacher, in an elite foreign language high school with highly motivated students and staff which truly is a dream job.

Put some Roots Down - Daniel Elias Galicia

Thriving in South Korea isn't only about saving a lot of money; it's also about making yourself feel at home in another country. It happens all too often when we move abroad that we settle for living in a scantily decorated apartment that feels all too temporary. But in order to thrive in another country you have to put your roots into the soil—bring your most valued possessions from home with you, put up some cherished artwork, cook at home and have dinner parties and movie nights as well as keep doing your most meaningful hobbies. If you make your home your sanctuary you're less likely to spend lots of money going out every night. It's cheaper to have friends over for beers and a meal than to buy a 10,000 won cocktail in a bar. And if your home is far more inviting than the nearest dive bar, well then you're set up for saving money and feeling deeply satisfied.

About Daniel Elias Galicia:

Daniel is a service manager for *Wall Street English*. He has lived in Korea for 3 years and is originally from El Paso, Texas.

Learn Korean - Lyndon Hott

My number one tip for thriving in Korea is simple. Learn the language. While I never was fluent in Korean, every effort I put forth paid dividends because it gave me a much greater degree of independence. When I first arrived in Korea, I was extremely frustrated that I had to depend on my co-workers to setup everything for me. Once I learned survival Korean, I was able to go to restaurants and have small talk with the locals. Koreans are always complimentary of any effort a foreigner takes to learn their language.

Learning Korean also allowed me to pursue my favorite hobby, hiking. I was able to research the best places to hike on Naver or Daum and where all the trailheads were. Because of my Korean language skills, I learned there were so many places around me that I never would have explored if I had depended on someone. Also knowing Korean helped me gain vast knowledge about Korean food and I found that dining out is a great way to network with your Korean co-workers. Even though I live in the US currently, I am still enamored with Korean food. Similar to learning the language, Koreans really respect foreigners who appreciate their food.

About Lyndon Hott:

Lyndon taught in various cities throughout Korea from 2007-2013, including Dong-A University in Busan and Dongguk University in Gyeongju. He is the former Vice-President of the Busan-Gyeongnam *KOTESOL* chapter. He's currently teaching ESL at a public elementary school in Fredericksburg, Virginia.

Celebrate your Favorite Holidays

Even though Koreans don't celebrate Thanksgiving and have different ideas of what New Year's Eve, Halloween or Christmas look like doesn't mean that you shouldn't celebrate them in your own way. Something like Christmas or Thanksgiving won't be the same as back home but get a rotisserie chicken, or a turkey (Costco!) if you have an oven and have a little potluck party with your friends. Plan a secret Santa event and exchange a few gifts. On Halloween, get dressed up and check out the expat bars which always have a party of some kind. It won't be the same, but you won't feel as lonely and sad as you would sitting at home in your apartment feeling terrible about not being in your home country.

Learn Korean Culture from Koreans - Kasham Laine

It's important to make Korea your home while you're here. One of the best ways to do this is to make friends with locals. Even if you don't speak Korean, body language, smiles and kindness go a long way. You'll learn so much more about Korea and the intimate details of the culture if you make a couple good friends with the natives. Only having friends from your own culture often lends to complaining about differences here, isn't so helpful in language learning, and doesn't allow you to fully adapt to life here. Of course, you should have some friends who are from your own culture, but those people shouldn't be the only people you hang around with on a regular basis.

Additionally, do make it a point to travel around and enjoy different parts of the country.

You'll not only gain appreciation for the beauty Korea has to offer but may also walk away with a new found love for what your home country has to offer as well. Some may find it challenging to do these things, knowing their stay is only temporary, but if you fully immerse yourself while you're here, I'm sure your experience will be all the more valuable.

About Kasham Laine:

Kasham has lived abroad for 8 years and called Korea her home since 2009. She's an avid traveler and has visited 14 countries. Exploring the world and empowering its people is her mission in life and she loves to share information with others through conversation, videos or blog articles. You can find her on *Youtube* (Kasham76).

Challenge Yourself - Lindsay Herron

Your time in Korea is a perfect opportunity to seek out new challenges, develop new skills, find new hobbies and interests, and improve yourself! I especially recommend improving your teaching; this will help you cultivate the respect of your fellow teachers and ensure that your classes are satisfying for both you and your students. Professional development is available everywhere; in addition to the workshops that might be required by your school or provincial office of education, there are a variety of online classes offered by Western universities and organizations such as the British Council and TESOL International.

KOTESOL offers many opportunities for personal and professional growth, as well. You can pick up new ideas and network at their workshops and conferences; learn how to do research and even apply for a research grant; observe other teachers' classes; publish your writing in a KOTESOL publication; explore your professional interests more thoroughly in a Special Interest Group (SIG); improve your presentation and public speaking skills; or develop a plethora of new skills as a volunteer or as a leader in the organization.

Of course, you can't neglect your personal growth, either! Try something new. You might learn how to scuba dive, audition for an English play, master a new language, take a cooking class, or volunteer. Pursue your passions—and don't be afraid to find new ones!

About Lindsay Herron:

Lindsay has been teaching at Gwangju National University of Education since 2008. Prior to that, she was a Fulbright English teaching assistant at a boys' high school on Jeju Island. Her new passions include presenting, learning, and leading in *KOTESOL*; discovering new tech tools to use in her classes; and scuba diving, which used to be *way* outside her comfort zone.

Volunteer: It's Good for You and the World - Kathryn Alberts

There were a few different reasons I started volunteering at orphanages in Busan. I wanted to get out of the city, see a new part of Korea, meet new people and try something new. I didn't initially realize how much more I would obtain from my experiences volunteering. Children who don't have a family isn't something we normally think about. Being an English teacher at a rather expensive academy, I spend my time around kids who have more than they could ever want or need. Seeing the kids at the orphanage light up when we come to visit, and watching them grow up over time is a very rewarding experience. Not to mention the deep friendships I have formed with other expats and Koreans who also volunteer each month.

If you are in Busan or the surrounding area, please join our Facebook group, "Busan Children's Homes Volunteering." We have regularly scheduled events that happen every month. Volunteering is a great way to be involved and feel much more connected to your community. My experiences volunteering have added so much value to my life here in Korea.

About Kathryn Alberts:

Kathryn has been teaching English to kindergarteners in Korea since 2014. She enjoys taking advantage of Korea's beaches, mountains, and cycling paths and truly appreciates the daily challenges of living in another culture.

Frequent the Same Places

In Korea, relationships are everything. This applies to work and friendship situations mostly, but it's also applicable to services that you use. For example, if you have a car I recommend going to the same mechanic shop all the time. If you like coffee shops find an independent one and go there often. If you like going to the bar, become a regular at one or two. Finally, if you eat out, go to the same places frequently. If you do these things and become a regular, you'll get lots of "service" thrown in, which basically means that you'll get free stuff!

Pets in Korea - Anne Marie Walters

Having a pet can make life a little sweeter in Korea and the country is starting to be much pet-friendlier than in days gone by. Koreans having pets that live inside and who are cherished members of the family is becoming more common. What that means for pet-owners in Korea is being able to walk dogs in the parks and beaches, more boarding places, and better availability of supplies and vets.

If you can make the lifetime commitment to adopt a pet, or if you bring your own, having pets can add meaning and structure to your life. It can also bring you into various dog communities, help in the lonely times, and get you out walking and seeing Korea through different eyes. Remember to adopt, don't shop—there are many amazing pets available in the shelters here or being taken care of by fosters. A good place to start is on Facebook at Animal Rescue Network Korea or Busan Abandoned Pet Sanctuary.

If a lifetime commitment sounds too daunting, there are still many ways to have a pet in your life here. Fostering an animal until adopted or until you have to leave the country can save a pet's life—many don't make it through the harsh winters here at the shelters. Another option is pet sitting; a good starting place is the very active Facebook group called Pet Sitting Network-South Korea.

A few cautionary words—make sure that the school where you'll be working allows having a pet in the provided apartment. It's better to be up front than to try and sneak a pet in because Koreans can be very intolerant of dogs barking. Also, look at the costs involved if you adopt a pet, especially in flying your pet home so that you know it's something you can commit to. As for me, I got involved in animal rescue here in 2011, and I am what is jokingly refer to as a "failed foster" because I fell in love with my dog and adopted him. Being involved in animal rescue and having a pet has brought so much joy to my life here.

About Anne Marie Walters:

Anne Marie works at a university in rural Korea. When not teaching, she can be found spending time with her dog Comet, traveling, and looking for a little magic in the world.

Works towards a Goal

Koreans generally have pretty low expectations for their foreign English teachers— usually it doesn't involve a whole lot more than showing up on time each day and looking like a teacher. So if you put a lot of stock into teaching giving you some sort of meaning in your life, well, you're probably going to feel pretty disappointed. And while you can make a difference in your student's lives and you should do your best to help them learn English, it seems like the happiest people here have something going on in their lives besides work. It can be almost anything—a hobby, writing a book, further education, building a side business, volunteering, or a social club. The key is to have a goal that you're working towards that doesn't involve teaching English and that can take up a lot of your mental energy and prevent the brain rot that can seep in from doing the TEFL thing for too long! The following three tips are some excellent examples of people who've done just this by starting a business, getting involved in the local sports scene and finally through creative endeavors.

Have an Interest Outside of Work - Cheryl Kim

The key to surviving in Korea is to have something that you're interested in or passionate about outside of teaching. Joining a group to do outdoor sports is an incredible way to reset and relax after a hectic week in the classroom. Korea, and Busan in particular, has excellent marine leisure sport clubs. Going surfing or stand-up paddleboarding at Gwangali Beach in Busan really helps to relax and revitalize my mind and spirt. For some, having a business outside of teaching is a welcome distraction from the tediousness of the classroom. By channeling creative energies and passion into a business idea, it has been very easy for me to survive in Korea both economically and emotionally.

About Cheryl Kim:

Cheryl Kim is a Canadian expat and resident of Busan for 11 years. Also, she is the co-owner of Kai Surf and Gwangali Surfing School in Busan.

Create Your Way - Kenneth May

Most of the old timers who have been in South Korea for fifteen years or longer have serious endeavors and passions they pursue in order to better the quality of their lives. My friends have become pilots and computer experts, bar owners, and savvy investors in global stock markets. They have started magazines, launched websites, published books, and developed their artistic abilities individually or with the support of artistic workshops.

A job as a university teacher affords a person a lot of free time. Twelve to twenty hours a week for thirty weeks a year isn't very demanding. Sure, a person can pursue professional development in the ESL field but the trajectory can sour once he or she realizes Korea won't always reward you economically for those efforts. ESL teachers who aspire to be ardent professionals often move on from South Korea instead of being trapped in a widening sea of mediocrity. Therefore, the folks who often have the happiest lives in South Korea are those people who think along the lines of, "I have great job satisfaction in Korea. I rarely have to do it." Although they take their jobs seriously and perform their professional duties in a perfunctory manner, they often have other interests which are the primary motors in their daily lives. Art is one of the leading interests.

Writing and painting are two of the most common pursuits for ESL teachers who have university jobs, partly because they are solitary acts which allow for a period of meditation and expression. As a foreign teacher in South Korea, one is always in the spotlight—in the classroom and in public. Not only does one have to implement effective lessons for students and learn how to function in a foreign culture, one must always be aware of cultural sensitivities and tightrope walk away from situations that lead to trouble, dishonor, or a trip to the police station. Even the most seasoned veteran of being an expat in Korea can be swept up in a tidal wave of unexpected events. Having an artistic pursuit allows an individual with the opportunity to step back from the "Quickly, Quickly" Korean culture and slow down, reflect, create clear goals, and work to achieve them.

Creating art is a process: idea, outline, research, creation, and revision. It's a healthy cycle for one's psyche and promotes individual growth and development. The serious writers and painters I know generally feel very content to pursue their chosen medium and define their identities through those efforts. With a sense of self-satisfaction already attained, they are liberated from getting worked up over the daily frustrations—professional and cultural—which derail many foreign teachers in South Korea.

In conclusion, writing and painting are by no means the only art forms to pursue. There are active comedy and theater groups and open microphone events too. Some teachers who have never told a joke onstage, acted, or played an instrument have joined those groups as novices and are now highly-skilled amateurs who may someday find work in those fields as professionals. A few are professionals already. True. Taking up an artistic endeavor is a great thing for an expat on many levels. It provides a mental sanctuary from an occasionally gruff culture. It promotes personal development beyond academic classes which can often be banal due to a poor work environment or uninterested students, and it can possibly serve as a springboard for having an entirely new professional life as an artist in one's selected field.

About Kenneth May:

Kenneth is a poet and event organizer from Indianapolis, Indiana who has lived in Busan, South Korea since May 24th, 1996. He founded the long time performance events Poetry Plus and Wordz Only. He will soon launch *poetryplus.net* and *kennethmay.com*

How to Thrive: Things to Make Your Life Happier

It can be really tempting when you're just coming to Korea and your main goal is to save money and/or pay off debt to get nothing to make your life more comfortable. I've been there and I spent the first two years in Korea living like this. Except that it's kind of miserable and I should have just gotten a few things that would have made my life happier and not worried about the little bit it would have cost me.

Get a Phone

In Korea you really do need a cell-phone. While a few of my friends have survived without, their lives were filled with more complication and stress than was necessary. There are plenty of cheap Smartphones with very basic plans for around 30,000 Won per month so there isn't really an excuse to not have one. Koreans love communicating via *Kakao Talk* (a Smartphone App) so you might be kind of lost without it; also, many social events are decided at the last minute and if you don't have a cell-phone you will miss being invited to join.

Get One or Two Nice Things to Enjoy Your Life

I remember my first couple years in Korea and how I bought absolutely nothing that would have made my life more enjoyable. Despite that, I managed to have an okay year but it could have been a lot better if I had gotten a couple nice things. Perhaps this could be a guitar, bicycle, desktop computer, nice frying pan, cutting board and knife, or whatever you're interested in. Here's a model that I think is really helpful for considering whether or not a purchase is worth it. It's an excerpt from one of my books, *The Wealthy English Teacher.*

"A helpful way to look at a bigger purchase is the **cost per use** model. For example, I recently bought a stand-up paddleboard for about $600, which is quite expensive in my world. However, I had used this item numerous times before while I was on vacation, knew that I was addicted, and also that I would use it a lot. Here are my estimates:

Cost: $600

Usage: 2-3 times a week, 6 months of the year

Total usage: 60 times/year

Cost per use, first year: $10/use

Cost per use, after 2 years: $5/use (based on 120 total uses)

Considering that the cost for a rental is around $40 here in Korea, the cost per use in the first year of only $10 is extremely cheap. I also hope to be able to sell the board for $200-300 when I leave Korea, which further reduces my cost per use. If I had only used the board three times per year, for two years, my cost per use would have been $100, which obviously would not have been a good purchase for me. However, at $5 per use after two years, it is a very good deal and an excellent frugal hobby, despite the initial high cost.

Another way to think about cost per use is **cost per <u>hour</u>**. Recently my friends bought a nice flat screen TV and had it installed on the wall. The total cost for the TV and installation was around $500. I asked my friends how much TV they watch and they laughed and said way too much, probably around twenty hours per week for the two of them together. Here are my estimates for their situation:

Cost: $500

Total usage/week: 20 hours

Total usage/year: 1,040 hours

Cost per use, first year: $0.48/hour

Cost per use, after 2 years: $0.24/hour (based on 2080 total hours of use)

Clearly, this is an extremely cheap hobby for my friends because what else could they do that costs so little, but which they are happy to do for such large amounts of time each week. If they only watched TV for one hour per week, clearly this purchase would have been a poor choice for them because the cost per hour used would have been very high."

Get a Car

While a car is expensive, having one is a huge step towards freedom and independence. It's easier than you might think to get your Korean license and buy a car so if you enjoy hobbies like surfing, camping, hiking, or sightseeing—it might be worth it for you. Since I've gotten one, I've taken some road-trips with friends that have been by far some of my favorite memories of Korea. Plus, it makes my daily life easier and less stressful—mainly due to not having to deal with public transport which used to make me very unhappy.

Get a Transit Card

A simple thing that will save you a lot of time and hassle as well as some money is to get a transit card at the bigger subway stations or convenience stores; it's only a couple thousand won. The most popular ones are T-Money and MyBee and you can recharge them easily anywhere with the little logo (they are everywhere—just look!). Another option is to designate your credit card as a transit card, which is what I did with my KEB one. They just bill you the amount at the end of the month. The best thing about using cards is that you get a little discount (around 5%) if you use them instead of cash.

How to Thrive: Physical and Mental Health

Understand Culture Shock - Josh Broward

Everyone gets culture shock. It's normal, healthy and unavoidable. It's also funny and annoying and depressing and depleting and confusing and sneaky. Sometimes you are having culture shock even when you don't realize it. Even the Bible deals with themes of culture shock. When the Israelites left Egypt, they complained, "We remember the fish we used to eat for free in Egypt. And we had all the cucumbers, melons, leeks, onions, and garlic we wanted. But now our appetites are gone. All we ever see is this manna!" (Numbers 11:5-6).

Another huge part of our adaptation in the culture shock process is coming to terms with a basic fact of life: there is more than one way to do most things. Even though my culture's way of doing things seems obviously right to me, it may not be right for everyone or the only right way. For example, Koreans tend to make and change plans quickly. As a Westerner, I value long-term, stable planning. But I have also learned that this Korean flexibility (which still drives me crazy) is also one of the key strengths which has allowed Korea to grow so quickly and to adapt so well to a rapidly changing global environment.

No matter what specific annoyances and adaptations you're facing, culture shock normally moves in a predictable pattern. As we discuss each step, I'll describe how a new Westerner often feels in Korea.

Stage 1: The Honeymoon Period *This is the stage when everything is new and beautiful and wonderful. You are soooo excited about your new adventure in a new culture. Everything is cute. This stage usually lasts between two weeks and three months.*

Isn't it cute how the little kids ask if you are an American? I love how the lady in the store just keeps talking to me. I don't understand anything she's saying, but I bought the soap she was selling!

__Stage 2: Frustration__ Eventually things aren't so cute any more. This is the hardest stage of culture shock. We can feel homesick, depressed, angry, and helpless. This stage can last anywhere from three months to one year. Some people go home while they are still in frustration mode.

Why does everyone ask me if I'm American? I'm Canadian, OK?! You want to keep pointing? I've got a finger I can point, too! I feel sad for those grandmas selling vegetables on the street. I hate when that lady at the store keeps talking and talking and talking. Doesn't she know I can't understand her? Just let me pick my own soap already!

__Stage 3: Transition__ You start to learn some things that are helpful. Maybe you actually start studying the language, so you can say more than, "Hello" and, "Thank you." You can use chopsticks without dropping food all over your shirt. You learn which stores have more familiar food. The key point in the transition stage is regaining hope. The transition period usually lasts one to three months.

Now, when the kids look at me in shock and say, "Foreigner," I point back and say, "Korean!" Instead of moving awkwardly past the lady in the short skirt hawking laundry detergent in the grocery aisle, maybe you try to get her phone number.

__Stage 4: New Balance__ After a while, you start to adjust. You find your rhythm in a new place and begin living in a new way. You feel less out of place. You find a few groups where you really belong. And amazingly, your focus begins to shift away from culture shock and culture and on to just living a regular life.

This is the best and easiest stage, but some people never get here. Some people just give up and go home. Some people here isolate themselves and form a ghetto culture within Korea. All their friends are foreigners. All their food is foreign food. Sure they work with Koreans, but once they are done working, it's like they live on a different planet, and all interactions with Koreans are unfortunate necessities. This is really sad. People who don't get to the New Balance stage miss out on many good experiences and good people. They never really see Korea.

Stage 5: Re-entry Shock You thought we were done, right? Nope. When we go home, we get reverse culture shock. Home isn't the same any more—or at least it's not the same for us. Maybe new buildings have gone up in your favorite park. Or maybe nothing has changed, and that seems incredibly boring.

Some people feel a great sense of surprise and betrayal when they go "home." Others feel deeply out of place returning to friends and family who have not had the same life-changing experiences.

So how do we go through culture shock with the least amount of stress? To deal with culture shock well, we need a few basic strategies.

Learn Become a student again. Learn all you can about Korean culture, and learn the basics of the language. At least—AT LEAST—learn how to read the letters. This will help tremendously with culture shock.

Balance Maintain healthy habits: sleep, exercise, and eating. They really make a difference. Also, stay productive. Too much free time becomes more of a curse than a blessing.

Community Build friendships and avoid isolation at all costs.

Home Figure out a good way to communicate with your family and friends. Learn how to get the foods that are really important to you. Put up some photos of home, and don't go too long without a visit.

Make it Spiritual We are holistic beings. Don't count out prayer as a realistic tool for dealing with change and culture shock.

Patience Have patience with yourself. You are human too. Have patience with people in the host culture. Have patience with the other foreigners. They are going through culture *shock, too.*

Culture shock is real and unavoidable. Culture shock can tear us up and spit us out. But we can get through it. If we address culture shock directly, if we are patient and loving and caring, we will find that culture shock can be something that leads to a kind of healing and growth and depth and community that is not available any other way. Engage the process of culture shock with open eyes and an open heart.

About Josh Broward:

Josh spent nine years working at Korea Nazarene University in Cheonan as an English teacher and pastor. He's since moved back to the US where he now works at Duneland Community Church in Indiana. He blogs at *Humble Future (www.humblefuture.com).*

Go to a Jjimjilbang! - Dean Brown

Jjimjilbangs and saunas are large public bath houses. Smaller places (usually called saunas) serve as a place to get squeaky clean, and sit in a bath for a short while. Larger places (usually called jjimjilbangs) however contain this and much more and are a fantastic Korean experience not to be missed. Basically, a jjimjilbang is comprised of gender-segregated bathing areas with pools of varying heat, a unisex area with sleeping mats, big TVs, PCs, massage chairs, snacks, and often a restaurant.

How it all Works

When you enter and pay (W8000-W12000), be sure to say 'jjimjilbang' to the clerk, as this means you'll be given the shorts and t-shirt set giving you entry to the unisex section. If you don't say it, they'll sometimes just assume you just want to go in to use the shower and bath, and then leave again. This costs a bit less.

Men and women have separate entrances to their respective bath houses. In larger places the sign will usually be in English and Korean, but sometimes just in Korean or Chinese.   or   is for men,   or   is for women. Some places will give you a locker key at the desk, but others won't. If not, you usually get it from a shoe locker by the entrance. Just put your shoes in the small shoe locker and find the matching big locker inside for your clothes and bag.

Now you're all set for the interesting bit. In the baths, everyone is naked. It can be a bit of a shock at first, and people have been known to stare, particularly if you don't look Asian. The reality is though that most people are simply too wrapped up in their own affairs to care about you and your bare backside. Don't sweat it! Disrobe, and proceed to the bathing area from the changing room. First stop is the showers. Everybody scrubs very thoroughly before getting into the baths. By the door there will be thin grainy towels. These are for soaping yourself up. Being covered in soap bubbles shows everyone just how sparkly clean you are, and is generally fun!

Now that you've rinsed off the bubbles, it's time to have a bath. In a decent place, there will probably be at least five baths. The biggest one will be cold, and you can have a little swim, as long as you're not bothering anyone else. The others will range from pleasantly warm to outrageously hot. Dip a toe in and check before taking the plunge! Around the sides of the room there will often be a dry steam room or two. A lot of Koreans like to hop between the hot and cold baths to get the circulation going. Look for any buttons on the walls, as these might start a jet of bubbles to massage your back or feet.

One more thing available here is a full body scrub. These cost around W15,000 and involves someone of your gender scrubbing EVERYTHING with a harsh exfoliating glove. In the corner you'll see a small price list and a massage table. Paying a bit more will usually involve a little massage too. If you want an actual massage though, I'd suggest waiting until after the baths, to see the masseuse.

When you've had enough of the baths, it's time to dry off and get dressed. Wander back to your locker and don your fancy shorts and t-shirt set. In the changing room, you'll find hair dryers, hair gel or hairspray, Q-tips and combs. Once ready, you can go to the unisex jjimjilbang area. Here you'll find all manner of things to occupy you. Usually there's a *masseuse, electric massage chairs, PCs, a restaurant or snack bar and some dry hot rooms for you to sit and sweat in. In a corner there will be a pile of sleeping mats and pillows. The pillows are sometimes wooden, and not great for someone not used to it. An inflatable pillow is an extremely useful travel companion here, especially if you plan on staying the night!*

Staying the Night

A common use for a jjimjilbang is as somewhere cheap to crash for the night after drinking or before going somewhere early the next day. It's not the most comfortable option, but if you can tough it out, you've just saved the price of a motel or taxi. When you arrive, take a bath if you like and then proceed to the unisex area. At night it will be a sea of people in varying states of consciousness. Find a mat and a spot, and get your head down. On particularly busy weekends, there are sometimes more people than mats. This is why I suggest keeping an inflatable travel pillow in your bag, or claiming your spot early.

Tips

-Bring an inflatable pillow

-An eye mask for sleeping is good too

-Keep some W1000 bills and W500 coins for the massage chairs and PCs

-Look around downtown areas and big stations for the biggest places

-Look for '24' on the sign, as most but not all are 24 hours

-The bigger, the better

About Dean Brown:

Dean is a long-time resident of Korea, and currently the owner of Springflower Guesthouse in Jeju. Visit *Springflower Guesthouse (www.gojejuguesthouse.com)* for details.

Find the English Speaking Doctor and Dentist

Even if you can speak Korean quite well and are trying your best to integrate fully into Korean culture and society, when you're sick or have a toothache, it can be really comforting to be able to interact with a competent English speaker. Chances are that your city has a dentist and a doctor who speak English—you can find them easily by asking on some of the groups on *Facebook*. For women, it's possible to find an English speaking gynecologist who understands western cultural norms and practices by asking some of the longer-term expats in the city that you're living in.

Use the Oriental Medicine Clinics

Whenever I have the slightest ache or pain, I'll go to the local oriental medicine clinic (they're everywhere!) for a treatment. It's partly covered by your Korean national health insurance so most visits will cost you about 7,000 Won and usually involve a combination of: heat, acupuncture, suction cups, electronic pulses and massage. It's very relaxing and way better for general aches and pains than something like anti-inflammatories. Even if you don't speak Korean, don't worry. Just point to your ailment and the doctor will know what to do. Or, ask the other expats in your town for a recommendation of someone who speaks English.

Go Hiking

Korea is a hiker's paradise—there are mountains and trails everywhere. Even if you've never hiked up a mountain in your home country, try it out a few times! You'll see some amazing views, get some exercise and see how Koreans really live. If you're alone, you'll often be invited to share a picnic and a glass of makgeolli or a shot of soju (remember—you still need to get down the mountain though!). It's kind of a Korean tradition, so be sure to get out there into the wilderness—it's excellent for both your physical and mental health.

Walk or Bike Places

One of the best ways to get to know your city is by walking. Even if other people think it's not possible to walk from point A to point B in your town, it often doesn't take as long as you might think. When I lived in Cheonan, I used to walk almost everywhere—to buy groceries, hang out with friends on the other side of town, to the movie theater and to go hiking on the mountains. It's excellent exercise and a great opportunity to think or just observe what's happening around your city. Another form of transportation that's perfect for immersing yourself in your neighborhood and surrounding areas is bicycling and the advantage is that you can cover much longer distances.

Exercise

Exercise is something that has kept me happy during my time in Korea. 5-6 days a week you can find me out running, hiking, surfing, or biking. There are mountains everywhere and plenty of bike paths in most cities. If the gym is more your thing you can join one for less than 50,000 Won/month. I think it's so helpful because living in a foreign country can make you into an angry person if you're not careful just due to the stress of not understanding the language, culture and some of the crazy stuff happening around you. There's no better way to take out this frustration than spending some time in nature getting your Zen on or working out some aggression by lifting heavy things!

Get Enough Rest

Something that happens when people go to a new place is that they want to do everything and are scared to miss something. Like they'll go on every single bus trip and foreigner tour they can find for the first month or two they're here. However, you should remember that you're not on vacation—you're actually working and have a job that will likely be taking up substantial amounts of your time and energy, particularly if you've never taught before. Keep this in mind and get enough rest. Pace yourself. Make sure you have some time alone at home, or with a friend or two so you can recharge and stay strong and avoid getting burnt out. Many of my favorite times in Korea have involved a casual dinner with a friend or two so if you're like me and don't thrive in big groups of people, be sure to make this a priority.

Practice Thankfulness

When you're in a new place that is very different from what you're used to, it can be easy to slip into negative thinking, which won't make your life in Korea as awesome as it could be. In order to maintain positive thinking, I find it really helpful to consciously practice thankfulness. This can be a more formal thing such as writing down three things that you're thankful for each day in your journal before you go to bed. Or perhaps, it could be something as simple as thinking about one thing in your head at a certain point in the day. Some things that I'm particularly thankful for about living in Korea are:

It's a safe place to live. I make enough money to live comfortably. Koreans are generally kind. Recreation opportunities abound. I can help people in my job. I have a nice group of friends. My sweet cats who don't ignore me! Living in a nice apartment. Seeing beautiful sunsets from my balcony. Family and friends back home. Quiet mornings.

How to Thrive: Shopping

While it's advisable to go "local" for most things because it's cheaper, if you need a fix of Western products here are my recommendations.

Iherb

Expats in Korea love Iherb. Even though the name is kind of strange, it's the best site for getting anything and everything Western. Some examples of things you can find are food, cosmetics, vitamins and supplements shipped to Korea from the USA. If you ever say to yourself, "I wish I had XYZ," search on Iherb and chances are you'll find it. Shipping is about $4 for up to about 15 pounds and there are sometimes free shipping offers as well.

Gmarket

Gmarket is like the Korean version of Amazon and they have an English menu option which makes it really simple for foreigners in Korea to use. Most of the stuff you find on there is cheaper than places like Homeplus or Emart. It's fast too and usually gets delivered one or two days after you order it. Don't be intimidated by the sign-up process—it's actually not so difficult and I haven't heard of anyone not being able to do it. Be careful, however, to do some comparative shopping since some things are really over-priced.

HomePlus

As far as shopping for everyday stuff in Korea, you have three main choices: HomePlus, Emart, or Lotte Mart. Of the three, I prefer HomePlus mostly because it's cheaper than the other two and they have a nice selection of Western products because it's owned by the English chain Tesco and isn't a Korean company. Be sure to sign-up for their loyalty card because you'll get some coupons in the mail every month as well as other deals and discounts. If there isn't a HomePlus near you, Emart is a much better choice than Lotte Mart simply due to prices.

A pro tip about shopping at these places is to look for the discount racks. There are always two of them: one for packaged goods and one for fruits and vegetables. The packaged good rack often has amazing deals on Western products that are close to expiring—I guess because they don't move off the shelves as fast as the Korean stuff. I've picked up delicious craft beer or big bottles of salsa for less than 1,000 Won. From the fruit and veggie discount rack, I can often find avocados or mangos that are perfectly ripe since most Koreans don't know how they're actually supposed to eat them!

Of course, shopping for stuff like fruits and vegetables is often cheaper at the local neighborhood grocery stores or markets than the places previously mentioned. One of my favorite small grocery chains is Top Mart because they have all the basics and great specials on fruits and vegetables. If you're looking for Western products however, this really isn't the place.

Costco

Costco can be a little bit dangerous for expats in Korea because it is indeed the haven of all things Western: liquor, meat, dairy, packaged food and anything else you could imagine. The dangerous part is that it all comes in big quantities, usually far more than a single person needs and before you know it, you've spent your entire monthly food budget and don't have much in the way of "real" food that you would normally eat on a daily basis. Trust me—it's happened to me more than once. However, it's fine to go every once in a while to treat yourself and get a taste of home but don't make it your normal everyday shopping thing. It's best to find a friend with a card and go with them (offer to buy them a pizza slice in the food court!) so you can avoid having to get the membership.

Alternatively, there are companies who specialize in shipping Costco products via *Gmarket* and *EZ Shop Korea* which I normally do instead of going in person. The markups aren't bad—around 20% which is okay if you factor in the savings of not having to get a membership and whatever transportation cost you would incur getting there and back.

Uniqlo and H&M

While I recommend bringing enough clothes and shoes to last you a year away, if you need a few new things I recommend heading straight to Uniqlo or H&M. They have all the basics in styles that most foreigners like and they also have foreigner sizes which makes it easy to shop there. The prices are decent and for example, you can get a pair of jeans for 50,000 Won, a t-shirt for 15,000 Won, or a hoodie for 30,000 Won. If you are a larger size person, the best bet is to head to Itaewon in Seoul where you can find "big size" clothing stores for men and women.

Repairing Shoes and Clothes

If you have something that needs to be repaired, it's really cheap and easy to do it in Korea. All dry cleaners double as tailors and can make basic repairs for you including things like shortening pants, changing zippers, fixing a rip, etc. If you need shoes repaired, look for the little shacks on the street corner and don't be afraid—the guy will understand you even if you don't speak Korean! All this stuff will cost you less than you expect and you can make your things from home last a little bit longer.

Getting Books in Korea

If you like to read, I recommend getting a tablet or Kindle and using Amazon. English books at the big bookstores like Kyobo are a total rip-off so try to avoid them unless you just like browsing. Some better options besides *Amazon* are book swaps, take one leave one places and What the Book. Most big cities in Korea have a book swap of some sort. For example, in Busan one of the expat bars hosts a swap once a month on a Sunday afternoon. Another option is that there might be a more informal take one leave one rack in places where you find expats—a bar, hair shop, coffee shop, etc. Just keep your eyes open and ask around.

Finally, What The Book is a physical shop in Itaewon, Seoul that ships around the country and also can import just about anything you want. Their prices for new books are reasonable, they have a nice selection of used books for good prices and shipping is fast and cheap. You can also check out the Foreign Bookstore which is about a 3 minute walk away from What the Book.

How to Thrive: Finances

For Banking: Use KEB

One thing that mystifies me a little bit is why any expat in Korea would use a bank besides Korean Exchange Bank (KEB). They are by far the most expat friendly and don't have all sorts of discriminatory policies that seem all too common at many of the other ones. For example, they'll give you an overseas ATM card and also a credit card that works with overseas websites, while many other banks won't. In addition, they have English speakers staffing their call center and designated foreigner branches where you can expect the full range of banking services in fluent English. In my experience, even the branches that aren't designated as the foreigner ones can do a decent job of handling requests in English and if they can't, they'll phone the translation line for help.

Exchanging Money

Most expats in Korea need to send money home at some point to pay their bills. Some tips related to this include:

1. Pay attention to exchange rates. If you have monthly bills then ignore this one, but if you can wait it out for a year or two, you can save a good chunk of money.

2. Send home larger quantities if possible. The fee, especially for your home bank receiving the money is often a flat rate so it really makes sense to not send small quantities like $1,000. I try to only send money home when I have at least $5,000.

3. Set up an automatic transfer system with a bank like KEB—it's called the easy-one remittance. This way, you can use an ATM to transfer money overseas, but only to a single bank account. The fees are a lot cheaper too. You can also set up online banking and do this from your computer as well.

High Interest Savings Accounts

If you're leaving your money in Korea for at least a year, it can really pay to set up a high interest savings account. It's simple to do this in any bank. The way it works is that you deposit a set amount (at least a million Won) and then leave it in for at least a year to get a higher interest rate. It can often be the difference between a rate of 0.5% for a regular account to 3-4%. It makes a difference and it's the perfect way to earn a bit of money on your emergency fund (see the next section for details).

Build a Small Emergency Fund

Once you're moved to Korea, you should build a small emergency fund. Ideally, you would have done this before you moved because it is always good to have a plane ticket and a couple months' expenses socked away in case things go bad with your new country or place of employment. However, if you do not have this, it is time to save up your first $2,000, which you will hopefully be able to do within the first two or three months of teaching abroad. I chose $2,000 because for $1,000, you should be able to get a plane ticket home or to another destination and then you will have another $1,000 to tide you over until you find work of some sort. I recommend keeping the money in a place that is easily accessible and by easily accessible, I mean available immediately in case of emergency, preferably in a separate bank account in your adopted country. Keeping it in your home country, but easily accessible with a debit or credit card is a good option too. Do not worry about earning lots of interest on this money because that is not its purpose.

Pay off your Debts Back Home as Quickly as Possible

For more details about paying off debts as quickly as possible, I highly recommend checking out Dave Ramsey's book, *The Total Money Makeover*. He also has a daily podcast/radio show (check the *iTunes* store), and is active on social media such as *Twitter*. I can give you the basics here which may be enough to get you started on the process. The first thing you need to do is figure out how much all your debts are and list them on a single piece of paper from the smallest to largest. For some disorganized people, this may be a bigger task than it actually sounds like, but do not get discouraged because it is vital to know what you are dealing with; an accurate picture of your debts is absolutely necessary for planning your attack.

Once you have this list, get into attack mode and go after the smallest debt first, paying minimum payments on all other debts and hitting this one with all the extra money that you possibly can. In order to get this extra money you need to be working nights and weekends, doing whatever you can to make a bit of extra money. You also need to live very frugally, eating beans and rice, rice and beans (I would mix in a few veggies for health reasons!) as Dave Ramsey likes to say for as long as it takes to pay off your debt. When you pay off the smallest debt, move on to the next smallest one and attack it, while continuing to pay minimum payments on all the other debts. You will keep freeing up more and more money as you pay off the smaller debts and then you can attack the bigger debts even more quickly. The snowball picks up speed and starts rolling faster as time goes on.

Sell your Stuff Back Home

Debt can be divided into two separate categories: debt related to a physical object of some sort that you can sell like a car and debt related to a non-physical thing or something that you cannot sell like student loans or medical expenses. If you have debt related to an object, I recommend you sell it, *immediately* and preferably before you ever left your home country, especially if it is a car. If you're only coming to Korea for a year don't worry about it, but this rule applies to anyone staying beyond that period of time. If you decide to return home after a year, you could buy yourself a cheap used car within a few hours of getting off the plane, so it is really unnecessary to keep throwing money into a depreciating asset (one that goes down in value) while you are overseas.

Save up Money for Life After Korea

Something that I've seen numerous times during my years in Korea are people who spend most of their monthly pay cheque, return to their home countries with very little money and no job prospects and then end up back in Korea after a few months, in the very place they said they'd never find themselves in again. Most often, they're very unhappy with their lives and would rather be at home but they just can't make it work. Avoid this situation! Saving up a nice pool of money for your future, whatever or wherever that may be, is something that you won't regret.

Get informed about Taxes

Educating yourself about taxes can save you a lot of money so it is a good idea to get informed about tax laws in your home country if you're teaching abroad. Check out an article I wrote on *Profs Abroad*: 25 Tax Resources Every English Teacher Should Know About. There's nothing worse than returning to your home country after teaching English in Korea to be stuck with a tax bill that possibly could have been avoided.

How to Thrive: Travel

One of the best ways to thrive in Korea is to get out there and see your adopted country. It's an amazing place and there's so much more to it than the concrete jungle that you likely live in.

Get Out There—Explore!

Korea is a very safe country and I generally feel far safer here than I ever did in Canada. Although you should take the usual precautions that you would in any country, especially if you're a female traveling alone, you can travel around Korea without too many hassles or worries. Get out there! Go places! See stuff! Even if you just got here and don't have any friends to go with you, don't worry about it and go anyways.

It's a pretty hard place to make a serious travel blunder and the Koreans around you probably have more money and nicer electronics than you do so the chance of getting stuff stolen is minimal. Koreans are also kind and if they see you looking lost and confused, they'll go out of their way to help you even if they don't speak English that well. It's a beautiful country filled with temples, mountains, beaches, rugged coastlines and peaceful farming and fishing villages.

Explore Korea, Solo Travel Style - Shannon Sawicki

Without a doubt, the thing that has enriched my life the most while living in Korea—and what has kept me loving Korea—has been my time traveling around the country alone. Korea has a vast network of trains and buses which makes it incredibly easy to get just about anywhere, even to all of the national and provincial parks. And you should go everywhere. Doing so requires a working level of Korean, a lot of patience, and the ability to laugh at yourself, but the rewards are innumerable.

I've missed buses and gone to the wrong places and lost hours and cried in front of strangers and miscommunicated dozens of times. But I also watched a bus full of elderly women giggle at penis statues and was offered a hot cup of instant coffee by the security guard at the penis park when I arrived there, bedraggled, on a cold and rainy day. I was invited by a coffee shop owner to stay in her cafe over Chuseok (the Korean holiday in the fall) when I arrived to find out that the campground in the park no longer existed; I ended up eating Chuseok dinner with her, and we danced underneath the full moon. An ajumma (older married woman) at a mountain shelter in Seoraksan asked if I liked whiskey; when I said yes, she pulled a litre bottle out of her backpack and poured me a cup! I was given a ride in the back of a police car to the next town over when I found out that the ferry service to an island I wanted to hike on had moved from Tongyeong to Gaochi.

I'm not sure I would have had any of these experiences if I were traveling with friends or if I weren't a foreigner. I definitely would not have had these experiences had I chosen to travel only to major cities or had I not studied Korean. Korea is a country full of stunning scenery, mouth-watering food (each city has its specialty), and the kindest and most generous strangers I've ever met. If you want to make the most of your time here, get on a bus and go somewhere new. Sleep in a jjimjilbang (sauna), eat the local food, and have a conversation with a complete stranger.

About Shannon Sawicki:

Shannon is an EFL instructor at Dong-A University in Busan, South Korea; she has lived in Korea for five years.

Go to Jeju Island

Koreans call Jeju Island the 'Hawaii of Korea' and while that may be overstating things a little bit, it is indeed a beautiful place that's worth a trip. Some of the highlights include hiking up Mount Halla (the tallest peak in South Korea), checking out the lava tubes, going scuba diving (look up Big Blue 33), visiting the sex museum (Loveland), trying black pig, and renting a bike or scooter to circumnavigate the island. A pro tip: you need to book plane tickets really far in advance if you're going at prime times (long weekends). By far in advance, I mean three or four months so get organized and go!

Go to Gangwondo

Gangwon province is up in the North-East part of Korea and it's known as the rugged, mountainous province with very few people. It does indeed have plenty of mountains with the most famous one being Seoraksan which is worth a visit. Gangwon-Do also has stunning beaches and the best way to see them is by car. Just drive along the coast and stop when you see something beautiful, which will be all the time so don't plan to go too far! You can also visit the DMZ (Demilitarized zone) at the very north-eastern point of South Korea which is quite interesting because you can drive into the area by yourself, unlike the one North of Seoul where only tour groups are allowed.

Go to the Countryside

Some of my favorite memories from my time in Korea have been when I took trips out into the countryside. Whenever I go to the countryside, I always return home, feeling refreshed and happy about my life here. If you're looking for a few ideas, check out: Andong (just not during the insanely busy mask dance festival), Gyeongju (a former capital filled with tombs and other relics), Buyeo/Gongju (also former capitals and very peaceful), or Boseong (beautiful green tea fields in the spring time).

Travel in Off-Peak Times

Korea is a very small country with a large population. This means that during prime times on weekends and holidays, it feels like most of the country is going someplace or another, roads are packed and traffic can slow to a crawl. If possible, try to get train tickets for off-peak times but if you can't, all is not lost. You can travel by road with minimal hassle if you travel during off-peak times. Try to leave before or after the rush. For example, go at 3:00 on a Friday instead of 6:00 when everyone else is getting off work. Or, come back on Monday morning instead of Sunday night if your work schedule allows it. I've had a lot of success in traveling by getting up really early—like at 6 am and getting on the road before everyone else. Korea really is the land of the morning calm!

How to Thrive: General

New Friends and a New You - Stephen-Peter Jinks

In a new country, other people's perceptions of you depend on how you present yourself, not on memories of past experience. No one knows you in Korea, so you can step up and be whoever you want to be. This is your chance to make a change. It could be as simple as a name change (asking to be called Christopher or Christine which you may prefer to the ubiquitous 'Chris' you normally get called at home), or it is your chance to find time for study or exercise. Or you could even turn a hobby into a business.

It can be lonely, living in a foreign country whether it's a small town or a big city. Meeting new people takes time, so instead of getting lonely—get busy. Being busy at work and being a good colleague is one way of making friends. The workplace is often a good place to meet new friends, but it's not guaranteed. If you want a busy and productive social life, you may have to look outside of work. A good place to start is KOTESOL, a professional teachers' association which has local chapters in each province. Professional development in English language education may not be what you are looking for in Korea, but it is a pretty good place to start because (i) you might get better at your job and (ii) you will meet other people who could become friends, or who could lead you on to other things like darts teams or book clubs or volunteer opportunities at orphanages or animal shelters (or anything). This might not be the kind of thing you would do at home, but your familiar home country life is not your current reality, so you may as well try a lot of new things.

As well as trying new things with new people, you can also try being a new you. Take on a new role and become the person who organizes the quiz night between teachers from local schools, or the clothes swap, or a hiking group. Get out there, do new things, meet new people and introduce them to the new you. Embrace the change.

About Stephen-Peter Jinks:

Jinks lived and worked in Korea for seven years, and he is now working on teacher training projects in South East Asia where he has lived in the same Malaysian small town for the past three years. You can read his language teaching and learning blog at *Language Spider (www.languagespider.com)*.

Strike a Balance between Korean and Foreign - Chris Ternosky

What you're about to read applies to both food and people. When you are going to Korea you might be worried about not having friends. Don't worry—you will make friends easily through your job, or just walking around aimlessly on the street. The first few friends you make can heavily influence how your Korean experience goes. It is easy to find a group of foreigners, and become part of their circle. They speak the same language, come from the same places, and like the same things as you. While it's fine to have foreign friends, you will have a better cultural experience if you make Korean friends as well. You'll learn so much more about this wonderful country and culture. The same goes for food. Eat western food every now and then, but branch out of your comfort zone and enjoy some amazing Korean cuisine.

About Chris Ternosky:

Chris is an English teacher currently living in Taiwan. He runs the growing website for English learners, *Learn English with Chris (www.learnenglishwithchris.com)*.

Get a Hobby - Pete DeMarco

For me, living abroad is about designing an adventurous and fulfilling life. If you want to experience the world you have to become a part of it. That can be tough when you move to a new country where you don't know anyone or speak the language.

I've lived abroad for almost 20 years now in a number of different countries. I was able to find work, make some great friends, and create enough great memories to last a lifetime. The main reason for my success abroad is that I find ways to engage with my adopted communities. My formula is to follow my passions to meet like-minded people. I try to get involved in something this is physical and/or mental.

Someone once told me, "The best way to get know someone is to sweat with them." I have to agree. I've played basketball since I was a kid. Whenever I go to a new country, I just go to the local court and play a pickup game. I don't even need to speak the language. In Korea, there are tons of outdoor clubs and activities you can get involved in: hiking, cycling, running, triathlons, bowling, soccer, sailing, yoga, and many more.

As for my mental activity, I love photography. I'm part of a local photo group that meets up often to go on photowalks and socialize. There are plenty of other options in Korea. You can join the English teachers association KOTESOL, practice your public speaking at Toastmasters, join a board gamers club, or take a Korean language class to name a few.

The best place to find these groups is on Facebook. Just do a search for what you are looking for. You might find some groups on Waygook.org. Another option is Meetup.com, although this is not nearly as popular. You can always just ask other foreigners too. Whatever you do, get yourself out there and create an awesome life for yourself.

About Pete DeMarco:

Pete came to Korea in 2007 and has been loving it ever since. He is the founder of *ProfsAbroad.com*, a job portal for university English language teachers. He also posts photos of his travels around Asia at *TheNomadWithin.com*.

Find the Realistic People

I mentioned in a previous section about avoiding the haters—those people who have a very dark outlook on everything Korean. Additionally, it can also be helpful to avoid those who see everything Korean through rose-colored glasses and will never admit to a difficulty or frustration about life here. The best people to hang around with are the realistic ones. They are mostly upbeat and positive but can share their frustrations without going to a very pessimistic place and they also have some sympathy for people who are having a hard time with something.

LGBT in Korea

Being anything other than straight can be tricky in Korea because many traditional, conservative cultural values still prevail and there's a large percentage of Christians in the population. While younger people are more open-minded and support things like gay marriage, these people are not going to be your bosses! If you want to survive in Korea (note: I only say survive, not thrive) you'll have to walk a fine line. Most foreigners in Korea are out to their friends and foreign co-workers but not to their bosses or Korean co-workers. If you truly want to thrive as an LGBT person and be totally out to everyone, as is possible in most of Europe, Canada or in certain parts of the USA, then Korea really isn't the place for you and I'd recommend teaching ESL in places like Eastern Europe, Japan or Thailand because they are generally more open-minded about sexuality. For more information, check out the LGBT resource section in the back of the book.

Commune! - Angelique Lazarus

*You're far from home, and that can be scary. It can also be one of the best things you ever do for yourself. Thriving in South Korea is more than doable. My recommendation? Aside from learning the language, I'd say a great idea is to find a community of like-minded people. Let's unpack the term like-minded people. As far as people, I mean expats and Koreans alike. As a Woman of Colour, I am very much in the minority here. Being a part of a community with other expats like me **really** helps to cope with a lot of the inevitable challenges of living as a Person of Colour in such a homogenous culture with a preference for paler skin (let's be honest). You also want to get to know Koreans for obvious reasons. This is*

Korea! Don't limit yourself by only engaging with other expats. I have really great Korean friends who are kind, funny, and helpful when I need it. Integrate! Remember: we're talking about thriving, not just surviving.

That brings me to this next part. What do I mean by like-minded? Pursue your interests. Find clubs or groups or events that cater to the activities and interests you participated in back home. If you are of a particular religion, faith, or spirituality, get involved with that community here. I guarantee you'll find one if you keep your eyes and ears open. To make things even more interesting, why not try something new? Is there something you've always wanted to do, but never did out of fear? Now's a great time to rip off that Band-Aid and go for it! Hey, maybe being so far away from the people who know you will make it easier. I find new environments can be very freeing. A person can really come into their own and thrive here, especially with a community of people with similar interests and challenges. Just remember to treat people well and your community will certainly grow!

A great place to start is Facebook. There are several groups for expats and Koreans to meet, for expats to commiserate, for adventures and new experiences, and more! As a personal recommendation for other PoC like myself, check out "Brothas & Sistas of South Korea" (aka BSSK) on Facebook. It's a great resource and a welcoming space geared towards the more 'melanated' among us. Happy Communing!

About Angelique Lazarus:

Angelique is an experienced English teacher in her second year in South Korea. She is also a singer and writer. You can view her writing at *Letters of Acceptance* (*www.lettersofacceptance.wordpress.com*) and *Pretty Girl ROK* (*www.prettygirlrok.blogspot.com*).

Find a City that Feels Like Home - William Mulligan

If you have been in Korea as long as I have (a combined twelve years) then it is essential to thrive instead of survive. There have been many things that I have done, but finding the right place to live is key. For the past six years I've lived in Gwangju, Jeollanam-do, and I am proud to be a member of its expat community. When the job takes its toll sometimes, I know there is always a sympathetic ear, or in most cases, someone to raise a glass with you. I am constantly surprised how much this city rallies around people, both in good times and bad. These are just some of the reasons why you will find people who have lived here for many years. If you can find a place that feels like home instead of just a place to stay until the next job, then you will have a successful time here in Korea.

About William Mulligan:

William has been living and working in Gwangju, Jeollanamdo for over six years. He enjoys spending time with his family and helping out in the community.

Live in Seoul or Busan

I think that most foreigners are happier if they live in Seoul or Busan (or another big city like Gwangju, Daegu, Cheonan or Daejeon). It's easier to thrive in a bigger city than it is in a small one and even more so than if you're in the countryside. It can be pretty isolating to be alone, without fluent English speakers around you if you don't speak Korean that well. Even if you can speak Korean, it's still pretty hard.

I lived in the rice paddies for five years at a university campus in between two small cities. It *was* beautiful and it had a large vegetable garden, campfire pit, BBQ by a lake, mountains to hike and rice fields to run in. Except that it was really hard to date and even meet friends other than my co-workers. Another disadvantage was that groups for things I was interested in—scuba diving, hiking, and board games—were nonexistent and since moving to Busan, I've definitely appreciated the broader range of social activities I can partake in.

If you Don't Like it Here, Go Home

If I had to give only one piece of advice, it would be this: if you don't like it here, go home. I always recommend that newbies to Korea give it at least four or five months to get over the worst of the culture shock and see what they think at that point, but in the end, Korea and teaching isn't for everyone and that's okay. If you don't particularly like it but don't hate it, I recommend finishing out your contract and making the best of it, but also make a plan for life, post-Korea. Under no circumstance should you stay and try to tough it out for another year just for financial reasons. You'll be miserable and a year of misery isn't worth whatever money you could have saved. If you're here for only a few months and every single day has been terrible, call it a day, break your contract and go somewhere else where you'll be happier. Bear in mind, however, that if you have a bad job that it is nearly impossible to get another job inside Korea if your visa sponsor doesn't give you a Letter of Permission to break your contract, and even then the next Korean employer may not offer you a job because you broke a contract.

How to Thrive: Home

Your living space is important because it can be your oasis in this sometimes confusing and stressful place that is Korea. Here are some excellent tips for making your home your own personal sanctuary.

Arrange your Own Housing

I lived in school supplied housing for seven years in Korea—two years in terrible places when I worked at hagwons and then a very decent place for five years. The past few years since I've moved to Busan, I've lived in apartments which I've found for myself. I'm far happier living in a place that isn't tied to my workplace in any way. Bosses usually make terrible landlords and having to complain to them about a broken toilet in no way fosters a good working relationship. In addition, your boss having a key to your apartment to enter at will is a terrible situation to find yourself in.

It's quite easy to organize your own apartment rental, but you will need 5-20 million Won ($5,000-20,000 USD) in "key" (deposit) money; most schools will not provide this. Depending on the deposit amount, where you live and how big your place is, rent can range from 300,000 to 800,000 Won per month for a place suitable for one person. You will need to speak some Korean, get a friend to help you, or find an English speaking real estate agent (bigger cities). Your school will give you a housing allowance if they don't offer housing but it's often too low to get something decent. In my experience it's worth it to spend a bit more and get a place that truly feels like a home. Speaking of real homes . . .

Make your Home a Real Home - Anonymous

The wisest advice I can share is to furnish your home sooner rather than later. Most apartments in Korea come with basic furnishings like a bed, closet, and washer. For my first year, I lived in an under-furnished living space. I didn't realize the extent of my own discomfort until my second year when, after investing in second-hand home furnishings (a couch, plants, an oven, cooking supplies, board games etc.), I felt like I was finally "home" in my own apartment. It was then that I regretted the year I'd spent eating off disposable dishes on my bed. Investing a little time, energy, and money into my living space offered a high return on my investment in happiness and allowed me to fall in love with the new home I'd made in Korea.

Your Apartment is More than a Place to Sleep - Marie Sorenson

Don't just use your apartment in Korea as a place to sleep—make it your home. Get a few pieces of furniture. You don't need much money to do this and you can often find very nice pieces dumpster diving (Koreans throw away the nicest stuff!) Spend a little money to add personal touches. Shop around. A few cheap frames for pictures, candles, throws, or rugs go a long way in making it feel more like a home and less like a dorm. Fill it with a few things that you love. For example, if you love art, get a few nice art pieces to add to the walls. If you're really into movies spring for a big screen TV. If home is about who you come home to, then get a pet. Many people have fish, dogs, or cats in their apartment. You want your apartment to be your refuge when you have a bad day in Korea. And on good days, it can be a place to hangout, have fun, and invite your friends over for games or drinks.

About Marie Sorensen:

Marie has been living in Korea for over eight years. Originally from the United States, she lived in Egypt, England and Hungary before coming to South Korea. Currently, she teaches at a university in Cheonan.

Learn How to Cook

While eating out in Korea isn't too expensive, it can still add up if you do it all the time. Additionally, eating Korean for all your meals means that you'll be ingesting way more spicy red pepper, salt and MSG than anyone should be taking in on a regular basis. I recommend going "local" by eating the basics at home—things like fruit, vegetables, eggs, and rice because you can get these things at the local supermarket and it will be significantly cheaper than trying to maintain a diet similar to your home country. Here in South Korea, you can get anything you could possibly imagine in terms of Western food, imported by Costco or other companies, but you will pay an outrageous amount for it. For me, it's an occasional treat to frequent one of these places and not my everyday mode of operation.

Learning to cook is really easy and a skill that will be extremely beneficial in your life, both in terms of living frugally as well as for your health. If you don't know how to cook or shop for food on a budget, don't feel overwhelmed, but just start by learning a few basic things and perfecting three or four dishes. Search on *YouTube* for "How to make _____." You could start with some simple things like an omelet, French toast, tomato sauce and pasta, or vegetable soup. Or, make a local friend and ask them to teach you a few simple dishes. Failing that, *YouTube* can work some magic for you! Search for "Food + How to Cook/Make." Here in South Korea, things like kimchi chigae (kimchi stew), pajeon (green onion pancake) or kimchi bokumbap (kimchi fried rice) are extremely easy to make and you can find the ingredients cheaply at local shops.

How to Thrive: Living with Koreans

After living in Korea for a few weeks, you will discover that the Korean way of thinking is really different than your home country. The sooner you start to understand how Koreans think and why they act the way they do, the better off you'll be. Here are some tips for learning how to live with Koreans—and not just how to live with them, but how to get along harmoniously!

Just Accept Things - Melvin

I came to Korea in 2011, found something special about this place and decided to stay. No doubt some of you have enjoyed the excitement of life in Asia. But I'm sure those moments of "culture shock" may have hit you pretty hard as well. I've also experienced it and I still find myself puzzling over the mind-boggling conundrums you can find here. The one thing I've learnt over the years is to never try and understand the oddities that make Koreans who they are. You'll just have to learn how to accept them (especially the longer you live here). Once you do, life tends to get a little easier and less stressful; the more you question, the more you'll get frustrated. I have learned to let many things slide. Another thing that I've done to help me stop dwelling on the numerous instances of cultural relativism was to start my own stand-up paddleboard business where I saw an opportunity to start something new and be a pioneer of an up and coming sport. It's lots of fun and I get to travel and surf!

About Melvin:

Melvin started Pine Ocean (SUP Korea) in June 2010 partly because the surf in Korea is so inconsistent. Five years later, stand-up paddling is becoming more popular and he's recognized both in Korea and abroad as the guy who introduced it to South Korea.

Reciprocate—It's a System of Favors

When foreigners first come to Korea, they often think that Koreans are some of the most generous people they've ever met because they're always paying for everything when you go out. However, when going out with friends there is this kind of complex system of reciprocity where it should all balance out in the end, even though Koreans might insist that they want to pay *all the time.* If you don't end up paying for at least some of the stuff, those people are likely to stop inviting you. A way that you can do this is to let your friend pay for the first round (usually dinner) and then you can pay for the second round (coffee, or drinks at a bar). Be proactive, get the bill and just pay it. Or, just keep asking to pay and the Koreans you are with will usually give in after the third or fourth time. Never try to go Dutch when you're out with Koreans because it's breaking a whole bunch of cultural norms.

Another thing related to this is that Korea operates on a system of favors. If you ask your co-teacher or boss to do something for you, they'll almost always try to help you out, but they're going to remember that favor and will expect something from you at a later date. While this isn't a bad way to operate, keep this in mind and try to balance out the scales periodically. Bring in some snacks or drinks to work and make sure everyone knows it was from you. When you go on vacation, bring back a little souvenir for everyone. If you're asking for help, give the person a cool drink to make it go more smoothly. These are all little things that can go a long way towards making your life in Korea easier.

Trust Your Instincts about People

I remember when I first came to Korea and how I would try to assume the best about every single Korean I met. Part of it was not speaking Korean and the other part of it was that I really wanted to fit in here. Over the years though, I've learned that just as in any country in the world there are good people who you should look up to, seek counsel from and respect and then there are ignorant and small-minded people. If you get a bad feeling about a Korean (or foreigner too for that matter!) that you interact with, avoid them in the future. Even though you might not share a language and you are likely not familiar with the culture here, it's quite easy to sense who the good people are. Trust yourself and your instincts about this.

Don't "Teach" Koreans about your Culture

Something that many newcomers to Korea try to do is teach any Korean they interact with about their culture, often starting their statements with things like, "In _____, we _____." In general, Koreans either don't care or are totally aware of your culture already because they've traveled abroad or watched American TV shows and movies. This mostly applies to life outside the classroom with friends or in social situations. The Koreans you're hanging around with probably just want to get to know you, relax and have some fun—they're usually not interested in a cultural lesson of sorts. You'll only set yourself up for disappoint if you think that your job is a cultural ambassador of some sort and that you'll be able to "enlighten" the Koreans around you. It's a far better plan to make it your goal to integrate into their culture.

However, in the classroom, it's difficult to teach a language without introducing some aspects of the culture along with it. My general rule though is to go heavy on the language and light on the culture unless there is a very specific reason to include more. Some examples of this are: preparing students for internships in the USA or helping them get ready for an English interview with a Saudi oil company.

Go out Eating and Drinking

One of the best things about Korea is the eating and drinking culture, which is often better than the experience we have doing these things in our home countries. Although drinking all the time is not a good idea, going out for some food and drinks with your Korean and foreign friends on a Friday night is a *really* fun way to spend an evening and an excellent way to unwind after a long week at work. Cooking your own food at the table is a bit novel when you're new to Korea and Koreans really know how to do it right with all sorts of side-dishes, courses and add-ons. It's cheap too and a meal of Korean BBQ and a few bottles of beer or soju can cost as little as 10,000 Won per person.

Learn to Love the Noraebang

Koreans take singing seriously and this most often happens at noraebangs (singing rooms). Even though you might not be good at singing (I'm terrible!), they can be a really fun time because you get your own private room, two microphones, tambourines and you can have food and drinks. There's a wide selection of English songs so have a few go-to favorites.

What about going to the noraebang but not singing? This is a big no-no and you should sing at least one song so that people will be happy. If you're terrible like me, find a friend who is a good singer and do a duet. Or, pick a song that everyone knows and is a crowd favorite so you can get everyone helping you out.

Read Books about Korea instead of Blogs

I know that everyone reads blogs these days and while there are a few good ones from expats in Korea including *The Marmot's Hole*, *Eat Your Kimchi*, *The Grand Narrative*, *Gusts of Popular Feeling* and *Ask a Korean* it's more useful to read actual books because you'll get an in-depth perspective that just isn't possible with a blog. You can impress all your Korean friends when you're well-versed in their history, culture and politics. Some of the ones that I've read over the years are and found informative are:

Cumings, Bruce. *Korea's Place in the Sun*

Cumings, Bruce. *The Korean War: A History*

Demick, Barbara. *Nothing to Envy: Ordinary Lives in North Korea*

Hoare, James. Korea—*Culture Smart! The Essential Guide to Culture and Customs*

Kang, Chol-Hwang. *The Aquariums of Pyongyang: Ten Years in the North Korean Gulag*

Martin, Bradley K. *Under the Loving Care of the Dear Leader: North Korea and the Kim Dynasty*

Meijer, Maarten. *What's so Great About Korea, Maarten?*

Tudor, Daniel. *Korea: The Impossible Country*

Winchester, Simon. *A Walk Through the Land of Miracles*

Job and Working Resources

University

Bolen, Jackie. *How to Get a University Job in South Korea*

Foreign Teachers in Korean Universities-Facebook

Profs Abroad (www.profsabroad.com)

The Chronicle of Higher Education

University Jobs in Korea (www.universityjobkorea.com)

Hagwon and Public School

ESL Cafe Korean Job Board

Footprints Recruiting

Koreabridge

KorJob Canada Recruiting

Say Kimchi Recuiting

Teaching ESL in Korea

Professional Development Resources

British Council-English Agenda

Cambridge University-CELTA

Cambridge University-DELTA

KOTESOL

Financial Resources

Bolen, Jackie. *The Wealthy English Teacher*

Hallam, Andrew. *The Global Expatriate's Guide to Investing*

Korea Exchange Bank (KEB)

Profs Abroad—25 Tax Resources Every English Teacher Should Know About

The Wealthy English Teacher's Website (www.wealthyenglishteacher.com)

Community Living Resources

Blogs/*YouTube*

Ask a Korean

Eat your Kimchi-YouTube

Gusts of Popular Feeling

Seoulistic's Living in Korea Information-YouTube

The Grand Narrative

The Kimchi Queen

The Marmot's Hole

The Seoul Podcast

Learning Korean

Korean Class 101

Talk to me in Korean

Shopping

Gmarket

High Street Market

Iherb

Whatthebook

Pet Resources

Animal Rescue Network-Facebook

Busan Abandoned Pet Sanctuary-Facebook

Pet Sitting Network South Korea-Facebook

Living in Korea Resources

Korea 4 Expats

Waygook

LGBT Resources

Busan Sisters (secret *Facebook* group)

Daegu GLBT+ (secret *Facebook* group)

Gaygu (secret *Facebook* group- Daegu)

LGBT and Allies in Korea (*Facebook* group)

Sappho Korea (secret *Facebook* group)

The Kimchi Queen

Utopia- South Korea

Travel Resources

In Korea

Air Busan

Asiana

Eastar Jet

Jeju Air

Jeju Island Travel Guide

Jeju-Springflower Guesthouse

Korail—trains in Korea.

Korean Air

One Weird Globe (Formerly *Chris in South Korea*)

Outside Korea

Air Asia

Air Busan

Asiana

Cebu Pacific

Eastar Jet

Jeju Air

Korean Air

One Weird Globe- Living the digital nomad life

Peach Airways

The Nomad Within

The Ultimate Peru List

Recommended Reading

North Korea

Demick, Barbara. *Nothing to Envy: Ordinary Lives in North Korea*

Kang, Chol-Hwang. *The Aquariums of Pyongyang: Ten Years in the North Korean Gulag*

Martin, Bradley K. *Under the Loving Care of the Dear Leader: North Korea and the Kim Dynasty*

The North Korea Blog

South Korea

Cumings, Bruce. *Korea's Place in the Sun*

Cumings, Bruce. *The Korean War: A History*

Hoare, James. *Culture Smart! The Essential Guide to Culture and Customs*

Meijer, Maarten. *What's so Great about Korea, Maarten?*

Tudor, Daniel. *Korea: The Impossible Country*

Winchester, Simon. *A Walk Through the Land of Miracles*

Made in the USA
Monee, IL
18 January 2022

89327067R00048